NOT
IDEAS

R. H. W.
DILLARD

FACTORY HOLLOW PRESS
a division of Flying Object

Flying Object Center
for Independent Publishing
Art, & the Book, Inc.

Factory Hollow Press c/o Flying Object
42 West Street, Hadley, MA 01035

flying-object.org • factoryhollowpress.com

Factory Hollow Press titles are distributed to the trade by
Small Press Distribution • spdbooks.org

Design by Pam Glaven, Impress, Northampton, MA
Printed in the United States
Flying Object is 501(c)(3) nonprofit art and publishing organization.

Cover photograph © Can Stock Photo Inc. / aopsan

For Duffie

ALSO BY R. H. W. DILLARD

POETRY

The Day I Stopped Dreaming About Barbara Steele (1966)

News of the Nile (1971)

After Borges (1972)

The Greeting: New & Selected Poems (1981)

Just Here, Just Now (1994)

Sallies (2001)

What Is Owed the Dead (2011)

FICTION

The Book of Changes (1974)

The First Man on the Sun (1983)

Omniphobia (1995)

CRITICISM

Horror Films (1976)

Understanding George Garrett (1988)

TRANSLATIONS

Plautus's *The Little Box* [*Cistellaria*] (1995)

Aristophanes' *The Sexual Congress* [*Ecclesiazusae*] (1999)

NOT IDEAS

by

R. H. W. Dillard

Philosophie dürfte man eigentlich nur dichten.

— Ludwig Wittgenstein

ACKNOWLEDGEMENTS

Grateful acknowledgement is here made to the following publications in which some of the poems herein first appeared, in one case (the seventh section of "Philosophical Investigations") in significantly different form as "In the Silent Secret Dark":

Mississippi Review: "In the Silent Secret Dark"
Pembroke Magazine: "Philosophical Investigations"
Blackbird: "Radical Primaticism"
The James Dickey Review: "Some Problems of Philosophy"

As my response to Ludwig Wittgenstein's remark that "Poetry ought really be written as a *poetic composition*," these poems form together a single effort on my part to write a sustained philosophical poem that actually *does* philosophy, that moves from investigations in a familiar poetic language through what Nietzsche called "philosophizing with a hammer" to an attempt to deal with a set of central philosophical problems in a pluralistic language that speaks at one and the same time in as many different ways as possible and, finally, to inevitable silence. Although they bear no blame for my failings, I owe very much in the way of courage and wisdom to my immediate pioneering predecessors, each in his and her own way a discoverer in the ways of writing philosophy: Lawrence C. Becker and Kelly Cherry. I am also deeply grateful to the editors of the journals who took the dare of publishing these long poems: Julia Johnson, Jennifer Key, Mary Flinn and Greg Donovan, and Casey Clabough. And, of course, to Dara Wier, Pam Glaven, and everyone else at Factory Hollow Press who have done everything to put this book into your hands. Again, as I've said and meant before, God bless the reader of these words.

CONTENTS

PHILOSOPHICAL
INVESTIGATIONS

PHILOSOPHICAL INVESTIGATIONS

1.

Goose waddle, splash,
In dark water, safe, looks
Back, long black
Stocking neck, opens bossy beak,
Actually two geese, in mind
Now, but then
(Once) in fact, fact.

2.

April morning, pearl gray,
Five sailing geese wing by,
One honking a startling bray,
Loud, obstreperous, not high
Overhead, curving an arch to day,
SSW swinging S, this cry,
This hoot, this feathered noisy say-
So soon echoed by another, wry
Vernal annunciation, airy essay
In renewal, electrify-
Ing aerial double play,
Goose to goose across the sky.

Spring indeed here on the ground
As well, daffodils, tulips, jonquils,
Bursts of green and yellow, red

And white, stretching earth to sky,
Exclaiming loudly to the eye
The goosey truth that just flew by.

And a splotch of brown, the woodchuck,
Newly awake from a long winter's nap
Underneath my bedroom window,
So delicately nibbling the first weedy
Grass, so mannerly, so alertly polite,
His brushy tail another bush
Bursting into rusty bloom beside
The scrawny yellow yawns of forsythia
Bobbing up & down, up & down,
A ragged seascape on the inland breeze.

These are some things to consider,
Things of this world (and we know,
Well-read as we are, what the poet
Said calls us to them), in every way
Worthy of investigation.

3.
Once again it's Peter Quince,
His fingers on the self-same keys,
Yet this time the tune is similar
But not the same. The clavier's
Strings do not jangle, rather hum,
Much like the bumblebee
Fumbling at the window screen

Its quiet longing, *Eine Kleine*
Angstmusik, a sadness beyond
Simple explanation, beyond
Philosophische Untersuchungen,
Beyond the window's sash, beyond
The screen, beyond the futile yearning
Of the buzzing bee.

               The metronome
Annoys and distracts me with its steady
Tick-tock-tick, but, no, not
The metronome, it is the clock
On the off-white wall, above the quiet
Calendar, the vibration of its quartz
Crystal defining for me (suddenly!)
What I feel, here in this room,
Desire.

       And what does time say
In its even measured way? That it is never
Out of joint, that we perhaps are out of time?
Does not joy always fail, it adds, sadness
Every time prevail? Tock-tick-tock.

Quick, says the bird, flown in
From another poem, Go, go, go.
In Word Golf only one stroke
From live to love, only one stroke
Back, bird says, be quick, quick.

Mehr Licht! the old man cries
As light surrounds him when he dies,
Never enough, *Niemals genug!*

                             And yet
From light to light, the young girl
Turns, and as she turns, a cymbal's
Crash and roaring horns.

                        Is not dark
Matter merely light compressed?
Tick-tock-tick time merely
Eternity's way of trying to hint
At what can never be spoken?
Always enough, *Immer genug!*

The room seems silent (tick-tick-tick),
The muffled humming of the bee,
Quiet click of the fallboard's closing,
Soft steps of Peter Quince's leaving,
The flutter of a bird's swift passing,
Hush, or you'll miss it, the last sweet
Echo of sadness ending.

                    Das Rätsel
Gibt es nicht. There is no answer;
There is no question. *Von Anfang an,*
From the beginning: more than enough.

4.

Three red tulips, you
Pointed them out, but
No bold-bellied bird
This time, only three tulips
In tilting late afternoon
Sunlight, a girl in a bright
Spring dress, yellow and bold,
And us, walking by.

Where is that bird? Where is
The reflection in
The glass door I was
Pulling open, then stopped,
Transfixed by what I saw:
You, caught so brightly there,
Fully in focus, by the day
Brightly lit? Both those
Images, are they a mix
Of memory, of desire?

Another day, another
Place, a drugstore greeting
Card aisle, a woman, thinking she
Was alone, smiling a smile
Of such unabashed delight
I was caught aback: what is
This place, this world,

That pleasure, so trivial,
So small, so silly, and so real?

And years ago, the day the world
Went flat on me once, no depth, no
Third dimension, as though it were
A photograph, each detail clear,
Precise and real, solid, even
In some ways seemingly solider
Than the rounded deep one
It had replaced, green grass,
White columns, wooden railings,
Walls of red brick. Which view was true?
And had I more than two dimensions, too?
But soon, in less than a minute's time,
The puzzles left unsolved,
The old world popped back
Into familiar shape.

The bird, your image on the surface
Of the glass, that private smile, the very earth,
Here one day, one day not, these are mysteries,
A metaphysician's lacquered Chinese box,
And add to it, too, that each time
I pass the tulip bed, tug at that door,
There'll be that bright (and missing) bird,
And there you'll be (and not).

How can this be, these things be,
Illusions; world, flat or round; this wonder?

Help me, Ludwig, now: "*Nicht* wie *die*
Welt ist, ist das Mystische, sondern
Dass Sie ist." Yes, yes, not *how* it is,
But *that* it is, this is the wonder.

Or this: "One might perhaps die of wonder,
If one could think hard enough over
The fact of there being anything anywhere."
More words, these are Dorothy Richardson's,
From her *Pilgrimage*, her pilgrimage.

More than enough, *miraculi* galore,
The mysteries of presence, mystery
Of absence, time's rickety tock,
Memories, desire, planet's dizzy swirl
Around a fusing sun, galaxies and ganders,
One cocky little bird ablaze, and you,
Waving from the walk in a shining door.

5.
Is this not the truth?
Night demands
The breaking of the day.

6.

"Is one then," Dorothy Pound
Once wrote, "only a bunch
Of memories?" meaning,
She added, "a bunch of remains
Of contacts with other people?"

Good question. Time
And memory, not that
Mechanical tick-tock-tick
But real time, space-time,
Outer space and inner space, Yes, mysterious time
Where we daily travel
And remember, river
Of time, time's arrow,
Old rollercoaster, creaking
Slowly to the top, then
The wild release, and down
We go, or time as freeway,
Crowded lanes, bottlenecks,
Off ramps and on,
And always all those faces,
All those voices, your hand,
Mine, contact, contact!

An accumulation of memories,
Piling up like stacks of glanced at
Magazines, is that it?

What one is?
Two geese by a roadway,
And all that followed,
Reflection, reflections,
Journeys, changes of direction,
Transom, staircase, glimpse
Of eager descent, a greeting,
Plié, jeté, quick flick of head, pirouette,
Slow turn of the head, smile
Of recognition?

Other memories, of course,
Accumulated imagery, bomb's
Shrill whirling flight, dictator's
Cocked salute, buildings'
Explosive collapse, thrust
Of the assegai, spear's flight,
Hiss of a missile's arc,
Cannon, small arms fire,
On land, at sea, and in the air,
The rattle and deadly boom
Of daily disaster, sufficient evil
Of the day by day?

Deeper memories, too,
Layered remains,
Salty lagoon, algaed bog,
First landings, crawl and wriggle
And hop, later landings,

Shorelines, new worlds,
Bootprint in the slick sand,
Flap of the planted flag,
Yes, where we are, scarcely
Remembering how we got here,
Looking for what we have not
Found, finding what we have not
Looked for,
Discovery?

Other ones, as well,
Sun's burst, planets' swell,
Syzygy, or slow spiral,
Leaves' easy turning to the light,
Bough's bend, rabbit's quick
Quiet, lemmings' rush
To the crush of sea, bear's
Grumbling scruff against
A nearby tree, fireflies
Aloft in darkness, alight
In deep boughs, dodging
Dance of moon, then sun,
Or moon and sun together
Across the sky, and wonder,
Always wonder why?

"Why can't we," Stephen
Hawking asked, "remember
The future?" Is it already here,

Always been here?
Or is it that the past,
There and here, and present,
Here and there, are quite enough
For one to know? And, for that matter,
Is one ever only one, or must two
Or more always be gathered?
Such gatherings, all this momentum,
Memory and fact, fact and dream,
Dawn, daylight, dusk, night,
One's trust in that progression.

7.
In the dark, invisible,
Is the rose red?

By any other name?
Röslein rot?
Rose rouge?
Rosa roja?

In a vase? A long stem
Wrapped in folded paper?
Held in a careful hand,
Or twirled by eager fingers
In the dark?

A rose in full bloom,
A bud, or one already blown?

Even in bright daylight
Or dim moonlight,
If the rose is red,
Is the rose's red,
Primary or secondary:
Objective, a wave length,
Blossoming of photons;
Or subjective, a sensation
In an eye?

And in the dark, unseen,
Is the rose red?

Man kann an die Rose
Im Finstern als rot,
Says Wittgenstein, *denken*
(One can imagine the rose red),
But I can imagine
That you are here.

In the silent secret dark,
The rose is.

8.
How we play at putting
Things in order, all in a row,
Eggs in cartons on a shelf
That extends itself along

The grocery aisle, developing
Thereby a syntax of space,
This by that, that before this,
This after that, placed
And parsed according to
Our grammar of things.

We tell ourselves, too, that
Time moves from left
To right, or so we mark
It, but didn't your eyes
Have to flick from right
To left to read those words,
Those lines? And isn't time,
Like the layout of a poem,
Quite as tricky, quite
As difficult to follow,
Define or understand.

We use a language
To try to describe time
That we first taught ourselves
Or learned from space "as it is"
(That's you), *"was der Fall
Ist,"* (that's, of course,
Wittgenstein again):
Words like 'before,'
'Between,' 'short,' 'long,'

'After,' as though we could
Actually amble or even take
A brisk walk, along time's way.

Think of Marcel, looking
For the lost in *le passé*,
Strolling gaily toward
L'avenir, or of Franz's
Worried Herr K, scurrying
From *Die Vergangenheit*,
Fretting toward *die Zukunft*.

We strive to measure it
In ticks and tocks, from left
To right — even those of us,
Or so we're told, who
Always read from right
To left, or, yes, it's true, up
To down — always toying
With that mystery, catch it,
Pin it down, observe it
A still life, measured,
Framed, that moving distance,
For example, two geese
In a snowy pond, this muskrat
Breasting upstream, mouthful
Of bitten green, in hot July, today.

So, yes, it *is* what is the case
That matters, whether matter
Immeasurably is what it is, isn't
What it isn't, or is what it isn't
Or is. Here to there is (tic)
Only one letter worth (tac)
Only one single point (toe)
In the games we play.

RADICAL PRIMATICISM

Our body itself is the palmary
instance of the ambiguous.
\- William James

RADICAL PRIMATICISM

Jungle cries, echoes
From the bone dry gulch
Of Olduvai:

Monkey business, the ancient
Ancestor, hominid, old Homo
Erectus, not yet sapient, that
Little bitty skull, dragging
His bloody knuckles across
The rocky shale, or her knuckles,
Old mother, and all around them,
Them, *OUK OUK,* a regular
Barrelful of monkeys,
Only they ain't got no barrels,
Yet.

The old ape in us, hair
Bristling on the back
Of the neck, that sudden
Burst of rage, uncalled for,
Unexpected *KREEGAH!!*
Display, the pounded chest,
Barrel chest, **THUMP, THUMP,**
Swollen forehead vein,
Bared teeth, those teeth,
Grinders, fangs, stained
Choppers of the omnivore.

NOT
IDEAS

R. H. W.
DILLARD

ERRATUM

On the Acknowledgements page, the Wittgenstein quotation
should read
   "Philosophy ought really be written as a *poetic composition*."

Or even worse, the brooding
Silence, poor monkey,
Monkey see, monkey
Stare unseeing,
Bored out of his gourd
Old chimp, jacking off
All the livelong day after day,
Whacking his meat,
But never learned to cook
His meat, chews it raw,
Sad fireless monkey,
Poor old ape, look what
He's growing up to be.

You may, if you will, shame
The caged chimp,
Smart as a whip but got
No swollen frontal lobes,
Wrong kind of thumb,
Improper opposition,
No elegant tunes to be picked
Out on the clavier by him
Just look at those feet,
They're only twisted
Angry hands, but before
You get too smug
Consider this:

What's the ugliest part of your body?
Asked an ad in an old magazine
That made apish men chortle,
Jungle cries, sure enough,
But the answer was, my friends,
Your feet!

•

But not your feet, not your feet at all,
So delicately formed,
Surprisingly lovely, in one
So slim and tall.

•

And consider this:
In California, Koko
And Ndume, signing
Their lives away, their clever
Hands, fingers flying,
Such questions, such answers,
Always looking out for
The nearest Coke® machine.

•

And Michael, RIP, so sensitive, the artist,
Saw his mother poached and killed,
Gorilla brother, died so young,
His pictures on the wall.

•

And consider this:
Washoe, she of "baby
In my cup," once ran away,

Climbed a tall tree and signed
The worst word she knew,
Long dangling fingers waggling
Underneath her chinny chin chin:
DIRTY, DIRTY, DIRTY!

Dirty indeed, our sister chimp,
The things we do, the things we
Do: those Asian dinners
With a course of live monkey
Brains (that are thinking
Which thoughts as the spoon
Digs in?); monkeys in the zoo,
Fixing each other's hair,
Scratch, scratch;
Gorillas in Berlin watching
Their favorite TV shows —
Kissing scenes and auto
Racing always pleases them,
Kissing, kissing and fast cars,
How closely akin; Barbary
Apes at Gibraltar, holding
An empire on their backs;
Poor spider monkeys lost
In space; the hurdy-gurdy monk
With his flat red hat; sacred Punjabi
Temple monkeys, snatching
Purses, knicking lunches, dragged
Off to monkey gaol; the wily chimp

At the Washington Zoo who lured
My dad up close and **PATOOEY**
Spat at him.

     •

    Better than the diarrheic hippo
    Who raised his rosy rump up
    Out of the sluggish water
    And let fly at the gawking,
    Ducking crowd.

     •

    But better for whom?

     •

Santino the Swedish chimp,
Planning ahead,
Calmly stockpiling stones
In the corner of his cage
To zing them at noonday
Visitors in a "hailstorm"
Of rocks and concrete chips,
Hjälp! Hjälp!

Tortured lab monkeys, our
First cousins, therefore very
Useful ("Here, Cheetah, have
A smoke."), like our other
More distant cousins,
Cats, stacked up in boxes
And vacuum packed
So lazy sophomores (not bright

Enough for Physics) can carve
Them up for two academic credits.

•

But not my Sheena, already burnt To ash and safely tucked away
In a red velvet pouch.
I miss her so
(You do not know).

•

Or think of the great Irish poet,
William Butler Yeats
And his monkey glands,
Requiring what ape
To became a ragged sack
Of bones so that Willie
Could get his willy up again.

A terrible beauty was born.

Or answer me this:
Why did Hitler, yes,
Sentimental Adolf
Who was bedridden for days
With inconsolable grief
When his caged canary died,
Why did he, the fucking Führer,
Order, in October 1941,
The import of 1,000 rhesus monkeys?

And a "troop" of Barbary apes?

To plant them on Gibraltar,
A hirsute fifth column, injected
With an infectious depilatory
To strip the Brits of their apish pride
In the way the CIA were later
To have a go with Castro's beard?

To do a little testing, a little tattooing,
A little vivisection, a little dental work,
Dr. Moreau, Dr. Renault, Dr. Mengele,
Maybe a gulp or two of poison gas
(You know why), or maybe,
Just maybe, just maybe,
Just for fun?

You tell me.

And now we must consider,
Those cinematic movie
Chimps, riding their motorcycles,
Or facing off with each other
In their little cowboy suits,
Grinning and doing back flips,
Trying so hard to catch Tarzan's
Eye with Jane in distress and
All the while biting the naked
Ape that played the lead

Whenever they got the chance
(Ain't that just Hollywood
For ya?), or leaping with ferocity
On the scared stuntman in the
Gorilla suit (voice squeaking
Out of the gorilla's permanently
Gaping mouth, "Get this fucking
Monkey off my back!"), oh yes,
We've come so fucking far
Up that old evolutionary ladder,
Uh huh, **_OUK OUK._**

All those monkeys
In that infinite philosophical
Puzzle, typing, typing, typing,
To be or nix to be, to be
Or mxyzptlk, to be . . .

Even the orange orangutan,
Dweller in the waving limbs
Of the very highest treetops,
Hanging on, harkening to
The din of axes far below,
Or, if captured, disassembler
Of all zoo cages, made to wave
(By Edgar Poe, who knew his cats,
Too, oh yes) a bloody razor, shove
The headless body up the chimney
Flue, or (What do you think

The orang thought of this?) tumble
On the beach in erotic foreplay
With none other than Bo herself
(Did he think she was a ten?),
Or, for that matter, ride around
With old Clint, not so old then,
In a freaking pickup truck.

The things we freaking do.

The naked ape that kills
And eats and eats and kills,
That eats and fucks and kills
And kills and kills, that's our
Natural sobriquet:

And we do eat, drink,
Solve problems, make
Decisions, speculate,
Theorize, economize,
Hit golf balls on the moon,
Run red lights, pick up
Hitchhikers or pass them by,
Scrimp, save, sacrifice
For others, care, love,
Hold each other close,
So close, roll over in sweet
Clover, make long love
All afternoon, all night,

Make war, make peace,
Bomb cities, bomb towns,
Cathedrals, villages,
Bridges, dams, roads, streets,
Temples, the homes of saints,
Masturbate, fuck,
Procreate, pray, prey,
Sacrifice, and kill, and save,
And kill and kill and kill,
Oh baby, just monkeying around.

·

Not you and I, we're not the killing kind.
But do poets ever kill? Oh yes, ourselves,
Each other, the stranger on the street.
We're dirty bastards, too, but we do try,
Don't we? We try, but even a poet, now
And then, has a bad day.

·

Our shadowy anthropoid
Ancestor, *mpungu*, haunts
Our waking dreams or those
That wake us in the middle
Of a peaceful night. The primeval
Beast of Cainsmarsh that cast
Old Herbert Wells into depression
At the very thought — "no ease,
No security, no comfort,
Any more," mind really
At the end of its tether — of that

Hairy face peering up not only
From the dim dim past but back, too,
From the shape of things to come.
Just as that same shaggy ancestor,
Dragging his cartoonish club
In one hand and his wife by her hair
In the other, drives desperate evangelicals
To screaming, ape-like rage
(The tell-tale mirror, to them, those eyes,
That brow, that grin, a dreadful
Thing to see, *KREEGAH, AIEEEE!*)

Display:
The scream, the pounded chest,
The bristled spine, advance,
Retreat, *KREEGAH,*
OUK, OUK, OUK.

Display:
Holding our ugly signs aloft,
Screaming at the crowd
Holding their ugly signs up,
KREEGAH, across the way.

Display:
Dogs straining on the leash,
Fire hoses, knouts, billy clubs,
Lashes, lances, fire hoses,
Rubber bullets, real bullets,

Golf balls with nails embedded,
Sticks and fucking stones.

Display:
The reddened face, the teeth,
The tears of rage, the screams,
And our great gift, gift, some say,
Of the gods, of God, the word,
Words that, some say,
Separate us from the beast(s):
You motherfucking shitlicking
Cocksucking goddam son of a
(Sputtering fucking rage) **bitch!**
Oh yes, display.

Trained carnival show chimps,
Caged in a sixteen-wheeler
With sides that can be raised,
Beating the absolute shit out of dumb
Men, maybe a little drunk, chumps
Who were offered fifty bucks
If they could beat the chimp
Or even stay in the cage with him
For a specified while (the owner's
Hands, with only six and one half
Fingers between them, counting
Those two opposing thumbs),
And the way the old chimp
Would size you up, rip off

The safety helmet you were
Told to wear, and beat the crap
Out of you with that, too.

•

No I didn't fight the chimp or even try,
But I watched, I paid my buck
And closely watched. I did.

•

Tears of rage:
Is there no limit to what
Hurt we will inflict?
Is there no limit?
Is there no limit?
Babi Yar, Katyn, Abu
Ghraib, Van, Darfur,
Wounded Knee,
Berwick, Gatumba,
Messolonghi, Medina,
Mountain Meadows,
Wolstenholme Towne,
Rosewood, My Lai,
Myanmar, Phnom Penh,
Malmedy, and worse
(You know the worst)
And worse and worse
And worse.

KREEGAH!

RAGE
RAGE
RAGE

Tears of rage:
Is there no limit to what
Hurt we will inflict?
Is there no limit?
Is there no limit?
Janjaweed, Danite
Band, IRA, KKK,
SLA, Sombra Negra,
Sendero Luminoso,
Hóng Wèi Bīng,
SAVAK, Hashshāshīn,
Al Quaida, Brigate
Rosse, Khmer Rouge,

Lohamei Herut Israel,
Mau Mau, and worse
(You know the worst)
And worse and worse.

KREEGAH!

•

What keeps a man alive?
He lives on others.

•

Jane Goodall's friends,
The wild chimpanzees:
Timid Olly, Mr. McGregor,
Spiteful Melissa who harbored
Grudges, crusty J. B., rugged
But gentle Leakey (Olduvai
Homage), David Greybeard,
Flo and her kids–baby Flint,
Young Fifi, and teenaged Figan,
So gentle, huddled together
Quietly near the nearby stream,
Cracking nuts with appropriate
Stones, with appropriate care,
Not quarreling when siblings
Take a share, consoling one
Another in grief, or pain, or loss,
There, there.

Jane Goodall's nightmare,
The wild chimpanzees:
The Four-Year War,
Drumming on hollow trees,
DUM DUM,
Biting off fingers, toes,
Pounding with appropriate
Stones, appropriate spears,
Chimpanzee war
In Gombe, that one awful
Female, so intent, chewing,
Chewing, chewing
The oh so tender flesh
Of that baby chimp.
Muncher, muncher.
There, there.

Our cousins:
Gorillas, *Gorilla gorilla*,
Gorilla beringei,
High flying Orangutans,
Pongo pygmaeus,
And monkeys,
Monkeys, monkeys,
More monkeys
Than you could fit in a barrel,
A hogshead, a firkin,
A butt, or even a tun.

Our closest cousins,
Sharing 98.7% of our genomes,
Chimpanzees, *Pan trodytes*,
Gentle most of the time,
Making tools for feeding,
Only bored and crazy in the zoo,
Roving in tribes, babies
On the back, eating berries
Or tacticians, moving silently,
Decoy, distraction, circling
Like Hannibal at Cannae,
Jackson at Chancellorsville,
Rommel in the desert,
Surprise, enfilade,
Attack, attack, attack,
And monkey for dinner,
Chewing and chewing.

And chimps hunted by men
For bushmeat, more men
Than chimps, many more,
Chewing, chewing.

Our closest cousins,
Sharing 98.7% of our genomes,
Bonobos, *Pan paniscus*,
The so-called hippie apes,
Peter Pans in Everland,
Never grow up, kids

Killing only time, gentle
All the time (unless you
Grab 'em), sharing food
With each other, with
Strangers, "make love
Not war," tongue kissing
In the wild, in the zoo,
And screwing, too, having
Discovered on their very own
The missionary position
Without the intervention
Of one single missionary,
Male on female, female
On female, stroking and stroking,
Petting and petting,
Rubbing and rubbing,
Fucking and fucking.

And we, so close to both,
No shock, then, to find ourselves
In such a fix, in such a bind,
Fight or flight, good ape,
Bad ape, the naked wonder.

Headlines:

PET CHIMPANZEE
BITES OFF WOMAN' FACE

NAKED MAN BITES, EATS
HOMELESS MAN'S FACE

A question for you:
What was it that awaited
Virgins who died unwed,
For centuries were said
To lead apes in hell,
To be harassed forever
By boorish apish behavior
Like those village women
In Kenya recently taunted
By vervet monkeys,
Grabbing their hairy little breasts,
OUK OUK, and pointing at
Their little bitty, *OUK OUK,*
Pink pricks?

"Admitting that the whole
Of a monkey is disgraceful,"
Reads a medieval bestiary,
"Yet their bottoms really are
Excessively disgraceful
And horrible."

By the way, what is
The ugliest part of *your* body?

And yet, there are the mysterious,
Elusive, quick, private,
Almost unknown, unseen,
Shadowy Bonobos
Flitting through trees,
Through thick jungle bush
On the south bank
Of the Congo.

And in the Congo,
"Boomlay, boomlay, boomlay, BOOM,"
120,000 lowland gorillas
Graze silently, always ready
To disappear again in an instant
In order one day to appear again.

•

O where is my wandering daughter,
Among the gleaners in the fields
Or in the lowland forests
With these gentle beings?

•

The poem of the apes
Is a poem of muscle, all
That blood from the brain
Drained to sinewy leg
And arm, gripping hand
And clever foot, stanzas of leap,
Stanzas of swing, stanzas

Of soar, stanzas, too,
Of wild careen.

Or the gibbon's eager poem
Of teetering delight,
On the end of a tall tree limb,
Her long arms spread in anticipation
Of her mate's hurrying, busy,
Rustling return.

> •
>
> Perhaps in Mogodoro
> On a dusty road filled
> With small monkeys,
> "Those little rascals"?
>
> •

Then there are those newly found
Missing links, the little ones,
Barely four feet tall. Are they
Our grandparents or did
Our grandparents — just try to count
The generations in between — kill
Or maybe eat them all?

Or were they just another
Missing missing link,
Perhaps no missing link at all,
Like our other grandparents,
The artistic Neanderthal?

Were they happy in the trees
Or walking slowly erect
From glade to glowing glade?

Or were they, too, afraid?

And what is it that we fear?

Koko in her safe sanctuary
Fears the crocodile,
Even a small rubber toy
Shaped like the crocodile,
Fears it in the bone,
Fears it in the blood,
Fears it in the mind.

What do we fear?

Abandonment.

What do we fear?

Abandonment.

Fear it in the bone,
Fear it in the blood,
Fear it in the mind.

What do we fear?

Betrayal, exile,
Massacre and torture,
The river running
With flesh, with blood,
The cold shudder,
The cold shoulder,
Closed shutter,
Empty shelter,
The serpent's tooth,
Enislement, isolation,
These people, those people,
The serpent's hiss
That whispers
In the dead of night,
Whispers
To our eager open ears.

What do we fear?

Abandonment.

It all comes down
Like dishes crashing
In the dark, cracked
Crockery all over
The polished floor.

The noise fills our ears,
As Joseph Conrad put it,

Like "a tribe of monkeys,
That insulting hullabaloo."

And that long flat space,
Distant, silent, drab,
Without boundaries,
Without doors, without
Windows, that empty
Space from which we
Watch the world
But do not enter in,
Detached, alone,
Lonely, and afraid:

Abandonment.

And yet, and yet,
Swinging lightly among
Broad cool green leaves,
After a soaking rain,
Patter and splatter,
A tribe of monkeys
Chatters like birds
In early spring,
A choral poetry
Of hullabaloo.

What do we fear?

Is it what
We most desire
(Afraid to have it
Or to hold it near)?

What do we fear?

The stumble, the stagger,
The tumble, the fall,
That which is the case.

Ecology of the Day:
Buzzing, blooming,
Vines that wrap and smother
The tree, limb that cracks
And falls, crisscross
Of passing birds, swirl
Of butterflies, hawk's
Deadly dart, swollen
Carcass of the deer,
Bear's lumber, crow's
Beckoning cry, crash
Of waves on the shore,
Teeming deeps, jungles,
OUK OUK, deserts,
Oases, mirages,
Crash of colors on the eye,
Spectra, sun's dazzle,
Transit of Venus,

Round on round and round,
Water, fire, earth, and air,
Such confusion, such
Assault, such chaotic
Order, part and apart.

Ecology of the Night:
Owl's hoot, swift swoop,
Vole's skittered squeal,
Skunk and Opossum,
Clawed feral cat, small
Things that move and shuffle,
Moon's transformations,
Apparent, transparent,
Shadows that shift
Or disappear, a filter
Of fireflies, shimmers
Of distant lightning,
Whisper of leaves,
Silence of snow, punched
Tracks, rabbit's flurried
Flight, coyote's paw,
How busy the night,
How lonely the night,
That startled 3:00 AM
Waking, absence,
Presence, alive, alone,
Alive, alone, alone.

Ecology of the Body:
In a balanced, healthy
State, 10,000 species
Of microbes in and on
Us, each one of us,
Separate, lonely,
But never alone,
Skin and bubbling gut,
Stiff bone, taut tendon,
Erectile tissue, oozing
Organ, bladder and liver,
Kidney and kidney,
Seeing eye, straining ear,
And busy busy brain,
Each of us, each one,
An entire ecosystem,
Swarming with pounds
Yes, several pounds
Of lively bacteria, fungi,
Mitochondrial organelles,
Together, all together,
United as one until
The final parting of the ways,
Final abandonment, final
Bulging, seething feast
Of auto-cannibalism,
That final obscenity.

Ecology of the Mind:
Not brain, whether
Connected, disconnected.
Interconnected, not brain,
Atop the brain (Descartes),
Perhaps below, intertwined,
Brain as organ of the mind
(Luria's conjecture),
Mind that observes, perceives,
Accumulates, assimilates,
Organizes, ideates,
Conceives, shapes form
And forms, formulates,
Formalizes, hypothesizes,
Mythologizes, theorizes,
Believes, achieves certainty,
Knows, knows, knows,
Only then to doubt, only
Then to disbelieve, only then
To give in, submit to inertia,
The solitary confinement
Of the tethered mind, alone
To commit the unforgivable sin,
Alone to despair, alone
To undergo the ultimate
Abandonment, alone.

What then is left for us to do
In this ecology of confusion,

This mental mess, this
Feeding on the inner self,
This thought-filled, thoughtless
Gorging of the rational mind?

•

What keeps a mind alive?
It lives on others.

•

Wallace Stevens offered
This solution, said once
Before he found
The palm at the end
Of the mind, of mind:
"Of what value is anything
  to the solitary and those
  that live in misery
  and terror, except
  the imagination?"
Shall we take his word?
Or perhaps other sights
At the doors of perception,
Hallucinations of the mad,
Absurd larks of the hypnotized,
Acid nightmares, opium
Dreams, shroom visitations,
Even the possible dreams
Of the restless dead,
I, there's the rub,

Dreams on the nod,
Waking dreams, dreams
Of the tossing sleepless?
Or perhaps what Peirce
Called "play of musement'?
Or perhaps what John
Cowper Powys called
"Dithyrambic analysis"?
Or perhaps what Werner
Herzog called "ecstatic truth"?
Or perhaps the very visions
Of the mystics, prophets
And the saints?

The poem of the ape
Is dappled by leafy
Sunlight, layered
Network of passing
Birds, drifting clouds,
Patterns of light
And shade, the poem
Of the ape contains
Long days of jungle
Rain, long nights
Of noisy silence,
OUK OUK,
Chit-chatter, high
Squeals, shrieks,
EEK EEK,

Screams, soft
Rustling of vine,
Of leaf and leaves.

What do we fear?

Distant rolls of thunder
Or are they guns,
Rattle and thud, loud **BANG?**
Poor chimp, hand
Ripped off by a poacher's
Trap, scabbed and leaking
Pus, hobbles, huddles,
Doesn't know he's dying,
Infection eating him alive,
Bloating corpse of a lowland
Gorilla, hands and feet
Lopped off to give some
Credulous Chinaman
A happy hard-on, oh yes,
The poem of the ape
Even contains the weary
Bars of its dreary cage,
The poem of the ape
Includes all of this,
All of this and more.

What do we fear?

Collapsing stars?
Wandering asteroids?
Magnetic polar shifts?
All our land floating
On a seething sea
Of molten magma?
Infinitely extended
Finite universe
That repeats, repeats,
Repeats? Infinite
Universe that goes on
Forever without ever
A stammer?
Mad tock and tick
Of puzzling time?
Does the poem of the ape
Contain all this? Should
The poem of the ape
Contain all this?

What do we fear?

What do we fear?

Suddenly,
I hear a gentle voice,
Melodious, as of
One singing.

•

Is this voice yours?

•

What does it say?

Fear not, the stone
Is rolled away?

Is this the voice
That nurtures, sings,
Purrs, enjoys
The passing moment
Of the passing day?

Every day, every day,
Birds begin to sing,
(They do, I hear them),
Twittering, fluttering,
Harmonizing their sharp
Discords all the livelong day,
Apparently ("apparently,"
I say) as happy as a whole
Barrelful of monkeys.

What do they say?

JUMP UP! JUMP UP! GET IT!

What do we have to fear?

What do we have to fear?
What do we have to fear?

Not a goddam thing.

There, there.

SOME PROBLEMS
OF PHILOSOPHY

The value of philosophy is, in fact,
to be sought largely in its very uncertainty.
B. Russell

Ein philosophisches Problem hat die Form:
"Ich kenne mich nicht aus."
L. Wittgenstein

Il faut donc un langage qui permette, à tout instante,
de passer de ce qu'on sait à ce qu'on ignore. . . .
Cette tendance du signe à se transporter d'un
objetà un autre est caractéristique du langage humain.
H. Bergson

SOME PROBLEMS OF PHILOSOPHY

1.

When the big dog barks
There are exuberances of caution,
All leaves on nearby trees atremble,
Birds' fear feathering, a dance
Of distant storm fronts, blast
Of limbs and trunks
Of falling towers of beech
And elm, of ash and gum,
Cherry and flowering dogwood,
All the whites of eyes blued
By a torturous afternoon sky,
Such independence, such
Slaughter, overstatement,
Exaggeration, hyperbole,
Language all atwist, words
Crackling like fallen cable
And wire, words scattered
All over the rigid air,
Texts and terminations,
All memories rendered
Into prose without repose
Or reposition, this whirl,
This chaos of order,
Of unheeded command,
Better, we say, to have

Let that dog lie but,
We know, the truth will out,
And so it will stay, or go.

2.

A strict imposture, words
And their stubborn shadows,
Orient airs, buzz and hum
Of accidental musings,
Inordinate strides,
Indifferent embrasure
Of rhythms beyond effort,
Such sorrow, such ditties,
Set your toe, stepping into
Time, treasure, walks
In sullen parks, dogs
And slips, oops, what
A day this has, overcome
By motion, take me
For a bride, eh, fat
Pants and envelopes,
Whatever suits you
May defer, oh my dear
Donkey, *quel âne*,
What a year this has,

Benjamin, Arthur,
Louise, ecru ectasis,
Is that a collar or
An entire suit, hearts,
Spades, broth ripping
Bellows in the lea,
Alee, abaft, baffled,
Beaten, butchered
And consumed, take me
As I, ay there's one
Of them now, snowy
Peaks, blank overalls,
Awls, hammers, slung
Like old masters
Lighting up, walls,
Depths upon depths,
Danger, danger,
Knocking, gaiters,
O Bishop, Saint, *ange*,
Give me a bone,
Buffalo perhaps,
Strictly imposed.

3.
The entire assemblage anchored,
In order, ABCDEFGHIJ&K,
Quetzalcoatl, plumage, arrhythmic
Entourages, LNOMTS,
Uvular, vexed, wistful,

The utter affair, all XYZ of it,
Embracive, columnacious,
Edictal, totally tiresome,
(The word 'bird' spoken
Slowly time and again and again,
The Promethean letters J, O, E, L
Notwithstanding) deceptive,
Misleading, mythologized, ergo
XIV imposes this mandatory stop.

4.

Abel was I or was I
Cain or Kane, a name,
What, in a name's
A rose contained,
In a sparrow hawk
A sparrow, in a shark
An ark, an arm,
Handsaw, swallowed
License plate,
Arkansas, Kansas,
Und was ist ein 'Baum',
Und was 'sehen',
I call you sweet but
Were you sweet ere
I saw semblance,
Eine Platte, flag
In flagstone, prey
In predator, a *rouge*

In *noir, ou est il*
Un rouge en blanc,
So much depends.

5.
Eudaemonic illiation, a tactile
Surprise, factive, factitious,
Ismic, such shouting after
Delight, impolitic, impolite,
Illusive illusion, indisputable
Tric trac, truth tables, tabloid
Disputation, *Alle Erklärung*
Muß fort, und nur Beschreibung
An ihre Stelle terten, primary,
Dies und das, the world is
Everything that befalls, is
That not so so, so intriguing,
Yes, sun's green, clouds
Red, *grün, rott*, bluegrass,
Hammer dulcimer, impish
Intaglio, says Wm. James:
Conjunctions, prepositions,
Adverbs play indeed the vital
Part in all, Ohoyaho, ohoo,
O say as you see,
O see as you say, I've read
That somewhere, bird, tree,
Stone, grayish white stone,
Layered black with faint

Gold glints, glints of mica,
Beside it, white stone
Flecked with tan, *Bräune,*
Solid enough to make
A scholar hop, thus, thus,
Always, always, *etwas*
Gänzlich Neues, utterly new,
Windows and doors open,
Holy, whatever befalls, new.

6.

Substantial confusion, perceptual flux,
What a mess to mop up, a sodden
Lump in the trash, eaches, everys,
Anys, eithers, no element surviving
From an earlier part, unlike it,
Forget it, shut off from it
By barriers and buriers, universe
Of discourse, noetic nonsense,
The sweet tender rich soft hump
Of the bison, tasty stuff, stuff,
Irreducible outness of anything,
Enigmatic Mona Lisa, fictive
Mona Dahl, Mona Freeman,
Such a youthful complexion,
Nature hat weder Kern
Noch schale; alles ist sie
Mit einem male, singular self,
Multiple being, *un seul fait*

Et une grande verité, action
At a distance, the curious
Stubbornness of fact, fate,
Fait, Factum, factotum,
Totem, ta ta, ta ta, tantara
Tara's ghostly halls, Higgs
Boson, link and bobolink,
Particulate multiplexity
More manifold than a fly's
Eye, God peering through
A billion, billions, trillions,
Don't blink or you'll miss
The show, *Immerland*
Πανταχή, come one,
Come each and every all.

7.

Umbrageous utterances, calculus
Of confusions without halt, undue
References, untidy inheritances,
A severance examined, contused
Calcifications, implants, infusions,
Insurgencies manned by disabled
Minds, *Seelische Vorgänge*
Sind eben merkwürdig, and that's
Saying a mouthful, buddy,
Get me, nabbed, collared,
Coming clean, coming clear,
Doubting each and every doubt,

Doubling down, both dorsal
And digital, humbly proceeding,
Merrily we do a sound,
Oh the depths and dubiety,
Stop, stop, stop talking
This inference, merely now,
Having owned almost nodding
To one's forebears, *Hilfe*,
Hail and *Heil*, a particulate
Farewell, *nous avions crié*
Au secours, but please allow
Me to continue, contained
And with cord cautiously cut,
Separate and separable,
To say what needs to be,
Implied and duplicate,
Das Feld eines Wortes.

8.

Abject mummery, magisterial
Maunderings, scribble, scribble,
Neologistic nonsense,
Another damned fatuosity,
Judicial, judicious, unwarranted
Benchmarks, mere caterwauling
On slack senses, come off it,
A thrown shoe, thump, thump
On a big base thumb, up or
Thumb down, what a scowl,

Such a caress, what cheeky
Kitsches, yet absence of umber
Umbrels, chill stillicides,
Unheroic couplets, and still such
Stolidity of ignorant opinion,
Unvexed views, unveiled
Prophecies, Tristram will
Never last and such,
How much better, lucky
Fly, to have listened in
To what Lucki had to say
To Frank on their Oxford
Patrols than to slog slowly
The great musty tradition,
Or chat of Moore and Stevens
Rounding the battery
Than to bear the boomings
And bluster of riled Harold,
Let us go then, you and I,
To the lake isle of runic
Rime, that other further,
Wo die Sätze klingen anders,
Wo die Zitronen blühn,
As otters ring the great blue
Heron's low, husky croak.

9.
Cerise claudication, clothed
In interpretation, contextually

Placid, *Ich ziehe ihr auch*
Die Deutung an, layered
Laborings, elephantine
Ellipses, callipygian
Callisto a major bear
In deed, steely Calypso
At home on Ogygia,
Caribs with their
Silent pups, knock
Knock, who dat, sea
Lanes and believings,
Say who dat, doggèd
Confessions, must we
Go on with all this
Hülle und Fülle im Reich
Der Sätze, there ain't
No other weight, no
Rime, no raisin, preach
And beseech, speak
And speech we must,
Wir müßen, nous devons,
As ρ must follow π
From this time furrowing,
I scream, you scream,
We all say and unsay,
Play and replay, ever
Tending toward λιμβο,
How low can you go,
Mirrored image of one's

Own mind, infinite,
Inner infinitude,
Say it, Josiah, image
Within image within
Image within image,
Time without, within,
Watching the watcher
Watching the watcher
Watching the watcher
1, 2, 3, 4, . . . n . . .
Infinite ingenuity,
Profusion of belonging,
Licensed or licentious
Erosion, exposure,
Explosion, extrusion,
Doing and undoing,
Longing and belonging,
Latitude and lassitude,
Who dat, what is she
Trying to tell us,
The this, the that,
The other, another,
The hurly, the burly
Of taut expression.

10.

Puzzled percepts avoid
A void, *wie merkwürdig*,
C'est incroyable, fill in

The blank, note that
Herr Weiß wurde weiß,
While *M. Blanc reste,*
Abysmal this abyss,
This abbess, these
Abeyances, black
Matter bulging empty
Spaces, this is how,
Mon ami, one packs
A poem, a case,
A rucksack,
A pig's valise,
A tome, an atom,
An empty stare,
Oh where is my
Vacuum, my Oreck,
My implorement,
Is everything just to
Fill up, a feathered
Fillip, ouch ow ouch,
Filigreed finials,
A final finch,
Sweet harbinger,
Where is my emptiness,
Only here do I see
Conceptual depths,
My multi-dimensional
Musings, as playful
And productive,

As piercing as Peirce,
Averse to pointless
Activity, seeing patent
Nonsense where once
Was only masked nonsense,
Ein nicht offenkundiger
Unsinn, old man's dreams,
Young man's vision,
I see the tree, the tree
Does not see me, the bird
In the tree seems to see
But ignores me,
Leaves leaves,
Flirts away, the day
Frilled with such glory,
Die heilige Heilige, les
Bonnes saintes, I see,
I say, I do-si-do,
I do, I do so see.

11.

Unbelievable activities, unseen
Sights seen, precocious, impervious
To insight or oversight, sawn
And dovetailed, dadoed didos,
Wheels within wheels,
Whales in the zodiac,
Scarves scissored
And swirling, high,

Heigh-ho, the merriness
Of multitudes, tunes
Popping out all over,
Organic, pedaled, pumped,
Hurrah, it's decoration
Daze, grave graves
Billowing with bloom,
Solemn sarcophagi
Split and sundered,
What wonders, what
Verities, what amazing
Installations, gentlemen
In their cautious shoes
And tied collars crying
No, no, no, no, no,
Keeping rime, rime, rime,
Unaware they're outta time,
Ho ho, the marigolds
So showy red, so
Flashy yellow, the doe
Wandering with her white
Tail aflit among the fallen
Trees, a fawn afollow,
Show me, the tidy lady
Cries, nosing her pince-nez
Through a cloud of witless,
Just look, just look
Where there's nothing else
To see, *ein wunderliches*

Sehvermögen, mystically
Mad, madly mysterious,
Yo ho, flow the moon
Down, warrened, warranted,
Manned, moreover over,
Let us calibrate this dusty
Maze, elaborate this twirly
Starred-over blue, examine
Cette vague vague, numinous,
Innumerable, unaccountable,
Mystiche, miraculeuse,
Illogical, irrational, this
Everyday, this now.

12.

Existential exercises, exorcisms,
Excursions, excoriations,
Hortatory exhumations,
Horticultural excises,
Ergo summa, theological,
All out the door so fast,
What are we to do
With all this *plénitude*,
This mysterious quinitude,
Quiddity, noxious
And obnoxious, solar
Absurdité, rien, rien,
Néant, nothing doing,
Not a ting go on, man,

Strabismus *douloureux*
Sore squintile, this seeing,
This separation, these
Splits and severances,
Excrescences, essences,
Loam *révolté*, sour
Flowers springing all
About *l'échafaud*,
La guillotine, you were
Perhaps expecting some
Reference to outsider
Trading, no, *non, jamais*,
A whirl, afflux, a fling,
All along the bored walk,
This extraneous shamble,
This closed examination,
The emergency exit,
A continuous clickety-clack,
Dodes'kaden, no dining
Car, only steady humility
While eying the other,
Wondering where the ending
Begins, all around the mulling,
The musement, the merry
Exclamations, exclusions,
Extreme unctuousness,
Overt anticipation,
This fullness beyond excess.

13.

Unassailable propositions, redoubts,
No doubts, zigzag ziggurats,
Auras doubtlessly scintillating,
Oh the pain of it all, dubious
Debilitations, philosophizing
Mit einem Hammer, poker,
Pow, kapow, kaput, kapok,
Experiential insulation,
Insults, sapid, insipid, salty,
Such wasted morsels, and yet,
And yet, I know what I know,
Nun, er sagt mir nichts Neues,
Ain't nothin' new to me, huh,
Down and out, up and about,
Verbal bouts, vorpal blades,
Kabam, kabam, alakazam,
You done it now, Houdin,
Who dat, Houdini, Houdon,
Stoneworks, breastworks,
Demi-bastions, redans,
Hornwork and crownwork,
Drills and traverses, reverses,
Recitals, recitations, receipts
And recipes, assaults
On fences, sensate, through
Bloody bone, circled seesaws
And tottering truths, I knows
What I knows, take it away,

Chop it, dice it, rice it,
I still got it, I do, forget
Verdun, forget Bataan,
Batter up, bubbling batter,
Battered down, unflattered
Tattering banners, band saws,
Sawdust, saw-toothed sawneys,
I saw what I saw, *du kannst*
Gehen, ohne irgenwo
Anzustoßen, browbeaten
But unbowed, bowed, buttoned,
Tied up, tried, taxed, tested,
Testy, clinched hand, the handle,
Safely out the door, R3, L12, R7,
To the street where the brightest
Lamp shines like polished steel.

14.

Appetitive apparitions, primordial
Prehensions, masked masques,
Harlequinades, what a lucky
Strike, pale faces in a shroud,
Done in, unrefined possibilia,
Misty reflections of a bright
Green spoon in watery plastic,
Illusions, delusions, unseen
Infusions, through and through,
Durch und durch, where to espy
The infinite, an easy answer

In the missing word, the blank
Space, *M. Blanc deviant blanc*,
Herr Weiß bleibt, so through
The domino, is that an eye,
An eyespot, an eyestalk,
An awkward emptiness,
Unspoken desire, desultory
Dimness, unsanitary manna,
Insane insomnia, oh momma,
What is it that you see when
You burn out the light,
Ein Blinder könnte leicht
Herausfinden, ob auch ich
Blind sei, then why do we try
So hard, the answer, *die Antwort*,
La solution, la bonne réponse,
Is at hand, the eye is the windrow,
Blue harvest *lunecer*, transitory
Idealities, ideation, ideative
Idées-forces, unglued and
Deglamoured, fact, fact, fact,
The barnyard, Mount
Katmai, Carmel, cadenza,
That mind behind the certain,
Nose that it gnaws, absolutely
Anserine, OMG, God knows
The face from the fat, the chard
From the glimmer, the gold
From the dust to dust, the answer

From the ants, my little brother
Quo vadis, evasive, divined,
Heavenward, home.

15.

Contranymic truths, heterodox
Hymns, he and she, sheep
In the meltdown, Janus
Equivalences, cleaving
To gather, cloven apartheid,
A this is just a this, a that,
A that, who dat say dat,
Dis and dat, *on-dit*,
Dese and dose,
Fundamental things,
Significant copulae,
Slithery propositions,
Erections, infections,
Wet stones, sharpening
Infractions, in space-time
Is anything just still, yet,
However, but, fixed
Motion, spirited influx,
Fluctuant understanding,
Does this $\equiv$ this,
Tabular truth, TTT,
TFF, FTF, FFT, is it,
Or is it this · this, or
(This **v** that) · $\sim$ (this · that),

Or this ⊃ that, wherefore,
Wickered sea of doubles,
Clonic yet dissimilar,
Splash, thrash, clash, trash,
Or make harm, is that you
Or possibly me I see,
Mirrored and magisterial,
Magical and *doppelt*,
↑ · ↓, ↑ · ↓, good fellows,
Puckered and seamed,
Curved, slid, forked
Like aspic tongues, espied,
Don't look away, left or
Right, southwest or northeast,
Hawked or handhewn,
Esse ∨ ∼ *esse*, self
Evidence, this ≠ that,
Inorganic or organic,
Or atomic, tip-toed or
Flat-footed, red shod
Or callous, the whirl
Is what the whirl is.

16.

Overt omissions, when is it ever
Necessary for one to twill the truth,
A suggestive Pilates remark if ever
I did hear one, a tooth in every
Yolk, each buttery biscuit, covert

Emissions or fragrant flatulence,
Every day I see, I hear, I feel
Dishonest disputation, *die*
Unwirklichkeit der Umgebung,
Lies, erasures, bent arguables,
Gott mit uns, Gott im Himmel,
Wohin, Gott allein wisse,
Graffiti on the Gordian wall,
~~Strike through~~ the mass,
Massive indifference,
Indulgences, unfeeling
Conclusions, that large lady
In the red cloche over by
The guarded door, is she
Actually there, *réelle, concrète,*
Solid as a crock, *komplett,*
Or a fraction of a long event,
Eventually valid, various,
Venous, a blonde, bottled
Or *au naturel,* or perhaps
Her hair is red, radishy,
Beetlike, bottomless
These questions, *Haben*
Sie Fragen, sagt Herr Schnee,
The former tennis champion,
From day to day, *Ja, Ja,*
Many damned *Fragen,*
Who said that, who dared
Speak up, speak out, demand

Something more, *etwas mehr*,
Not me, boy, no way, just
Minding my own busyness,
Where, then, do we turn,
Where does the truth lie
Down, you tell me, pal,
And then we'll both know.

17.

La bonheur, *die Glück*, happiness,
Pursuit of same, two whales
Crossing a bar, M. Blanc, Herr Weiss,
So then Blanc *dit* to Weiss,
Who dat following me around,
Old one-peggèd man in a hot hurry,
Then *sagt* Weiss to Blanc,
Who dat say who dat, ho ho,
Dit Blanc to Weiss, *ouf*,
Peuh, that's one on me, *aïe*,
Help, *le bon Dieu*, *le Seigneur*
Dieu, how does one, *c'est moi*,
Seek after the happitude, sound
Out the syllabi, scotch the syllabub,
Try out 'happy' to mean 'sad,'
'Sad' to mean 'happy,' could it
Be done, I'm so sad I could
Cry, I'm so happy I could die,
Is this *Sprachspiel* even possible,
Inalienable, unavailable, veiled

In tears, vase of fears, sheer luck,
Good and bad, lucky and plucky,
Stars, planets, planetoids,
Planetaria, planaria, pure
Sense, sure nonsense,
An august augury, evil,
Le mal, die Übel, is mere
Absence, *néant*, no good,
Or is that the other way
Around, *Güte, bienveillance*,
An emptiness of ubiquitous
Evil, force of badness, rife
Ripening, how am I to be
Happy when I am not good,
Am not humble, virtue
That dare not say its name,
Am infernally mordant, yet
Laughing all the way, polly
Wolly doodling, popping
Perps, prepping peeps,
Give me a break, huh, step
Aside, there's *Nichts* to see
Here, nix, no dice, *niemals*,
Jamais, oh to be unangled
Now that I finally may, hopping,
Hoping, shelving and extending
A handy swipe or two or more,
Clean as a viper's tooth, washed
Windows and opening doors,

All the way to the edge, a peep
At the whole, beyond the restive,
The festive, the gala, *die Schrift*,
Runic and ruminative, like kine
In the roiling lea, kerploppity,
Goodness knows, I have no
Idea, no idiom, no identity
Beyond this exact and perfect,
Momentous and mooing,
Magnificent and morate,
Nowhere never, here and new,
At hand, *hierbeikommen*,
Inwendig, within, without,
Now and forever, amends.

18.

Hormic haruspex, dabbling in the dark,
Spilt innards, no longer lively vitals,
What's that coming down the road,
What road, pray tell, is that, wrong
And grinding perhaps, rosemaried
And thymed, how does one such who
Meets another keep from laughing,
Also sprach Cato once upon a time
Past, ghost of things yet to come,
Rattle dem bones, juggle dem guts,
Roule dem dice, *bon temps ou mal*,
Plaqued fingertips, wispy voices,
Letter by *lettre, nicht in alphabetischer*

Reihenfolge, massages from beyond,
Rolfed and battered, soothfast or
Soothing, mendacious or mendicant,
Oui, Ja, Non, Nein, to not or to know,
The flights and scries of birds,
Bustard bluster, flighty *pink*
Of the bobolink, what is that iterative
Linkalinkalink, a flickering flit
Through those sheltering lives,
Surely a crucial crux, a crisis
In the ofting, a feathery fract,
Clouds, moles, numinous numbers,
Major and minor prophets,
Great and lesser bearings, lines
Between stares, a stairway
To paradise, or just another
Tumor, matters of strife
And rest, are you getting it,
Reading the ruins, decoding
The sighs and cymbali,
Stumps and stumbles, cracks
Crisscross the pavement, hats
Abed, bedazzled, baffled,
Begrudging, embattled, beat,
Toss dem yarrow stalks,
Dem holey coinage, long
Lines and short, but you
Must pay at the counter,
Synchronous syllables,

Signals from the safety
Coffin, angels in the infield,
Oh my friend, *mon ami*,
Mein Freund, even *Herr*
Doktor Traumleser him
Very *selbst*, let us hold
Hands in unbroken circus,
A clownish *plausūs* or so,
Singalingaling, a rumpled
Chorus, leggy chorines
Atwitter, a splutter
Of predication, predictive
Splinters, tomorrow is
What the marrow zings,
Eyes lidded down while
Climbing up the hill,
Baring a baleful pailful,
Blind as a gnat, glad
As a blimp, simple
Without simony, taking
What becomes, slowly
Or lickety-splickety, but
No, nay, never, no nay
Never no more, will you
Pass the day over,
Nor never let go.

19.

Purplish prehensions, all dolled up
In fancy dancy language, gobbled
Jug bands, jargonized jibberjabber,
Shells and seashells, Seychelles,
Sur la plage, sifting sounds
And carbonized palaver,
Conceptual dibbledabble,
Extensive irrelevancies, seed
Pods, hollowed and hallowed,
Shiny surfaces, no deep diving
Allowed, shallow waders,
Dams and weirs, mired sludge
And sheer fudge, where's
That genius gone, washed out
By truncheons and knouts,
Impolitic corrections, bans
And steel bands, chained
Links, tied tongues, where's
That useful clipper, medial
Snipper, enough of this
Baloney, ornery orbiting,
Round and round the out
House, *Scheißengebäude*,
Where's that hell of a good
Universe anyhow, inflated
Inflaton, *Nebenweltall*,
Why am I so cranked up
And cranky, what's eating

My apples, my verbal
Be all, bee hive, behemoth,
Bucolic be and be, nestled
Silky spider's webbing,
And what's that roister,
Shakespeherian chuckles,
Loud and out larfter, mate,
Bebouncing all the way,
Anchors aweighed, up and go,
Out of this messed up morass,
Goofy gibblegabble,
These challenges dressed
In furry lingo, leery
Lingua, lexical tar pit,
Fossilized flapdoodle,
Break on through, make
A break, head for the nigh
Ground, enough of this
Flustration, flattered
Fibulation, pointless
Piffle, *Zu Hilfe kommen*, Ludwig,
Worte eines Dichters können uns
Durch und durch gehen,
Let us roam up and down
In die wohlbekannte Umgebung
Der Worte, woodlands aring
With mockingbird multiplex
Song, bronze Brahms, *Andante*,
Opus 67, pallid Pallas, *l'esprit*

Disparu, firefangled fathers,
Think and be whole again,
Beyond confutation, stolid
Walls and windows, miracles
And mirrors, *das treffunde Wort*.

20.

Esurient escalations, prehensile
Grabblings, jimmied gimmes,
I, me, mine, such much and more,
Mined all mined, can you
Dig it, anthropocentric krazies,
Copped feels and fetid graspings,
Hugger-muggered loot, louvered
Ransoms, loggy undoers, what
A fracked up mess, doncha know,
Every hand in every itching
Ta-pocketa-pocketa-pocketa,
Cold fingered and undemitted,
Parlous, heedless, bland
Bleeding the bland, why you,
So ostensible, offensible, fenced
In, impostured enclosures, doncha
See what's ondoing, downgoing,
As the seised wries, toroid tornadoes
Dewreck de righteous, bullions
In the offshore and flat-tired
Taxis, do you even know where
You are, is that an eyeful or am I

Kwazy as a doozy, and you,
Adoze and adaft, why do I
Go on this way, *wenn ich sage,*
Was ich weiß, – wie sage ich
<u>Das</u>, *was ich weiß,* ever defter
And denser, all ten stringy
Delusional dimensions
Needed to make the math work
Out, right enough or so,
All that, too much, unknown,
Unseen, you say, so say nothing,
You say, grub everything within
Harm's wracked wrench, trust
Graven Job creators to give
You just what you asked for,
Well deserved desserts, so
What's my problem, huh,
You're asking that for sure,
Why can't I just taste brass
Tacks, be lingually bereft,
Nun, ich kann es nicht
Anders ausdrücken, too bad
For you, but hang on for
Half a mo, a triple sec,
Just one more shot, *eine Frage,*
If you will, *un quête de*
La vérité, M. Bain de Boue,
Pourquoi, warum, Herr Verwirrung,
Do you trick trek so far for Ophir

Or Opar or any such other
Ophidian Orcades, take a gander
At panning for this slipsloshed
Solvency, land of bilk and funny
Money, dangle jingle jangle
In the old pants pocket, when you
Already have all the doodah,
Dits, dots and crosses, ducks
And does, sufficient thereto
Unto all the livelong day.

21.

What is it that you see, the seen
Scene, the ostensive essential,
The stubborn tract, not suborned
Fascicles, but better the kicked rock,
The battered bustle, heard knocks,
The eked acre, or is the the the a,
An answering echo, pointillist
Composure, this, this, this,
Rot ist eben dies, *und bitter* dies,
Und Schmerz dies, pained hand,
Schuldige Schulter, knocked
Knee, red, bitter, and sore,
Thoreau in the fog, *Contact*,
Contact, Wittgenstein in the dark,
Die Geräusch, die Geratter
Des Regens, in the very face
Of spattered splattering, *jetzt*

Und nun, fracture of spacetime,
Driblet of singular duplicity,
Implacable was, is, will be,
Matter abuzz with material
Density, intensity, immensity,
This rap on the noggin, ouch
Of eternity, hardy and heartfelt,
Of other, *ander*, *autre*, one, one
And one, now, altogether now,
Monomatrix, do you ever know
What is yours, only getting by,
Unfeeling time, timid, spry,
Whirling stability, mangered
Mainstay, mended certainties,
I seize what I see, I know
What eye knows, mindful
Wall at the end of solar wind,
Mingled mutterings, mutations,
And yet, and yet, wood, wold,
Would, woad, black and blues,
Days and noughts, electric sheen,
Eclectic shine, a sensible
Here, the present, there,
Gifted, given, the A
In *Absurdität*, the a
In appellation, the *a* in *aperçu*,
The a in all in all.

22.

Deafen the difference, interrogation
And explanation, interrogative
Expletive, engrammatical ecstasy,
Graven finial joists, are you
Asking me or telling me, over there,
The inherence, outer to inner,
Enter to utterance, mourning
To moose calls, is that a train
Coming, a stain on the moaning
Air, a violinist or a misfit,
Passage or tumescence,
These are turpentinic turpitudes,
Denatured, argumentative,
Ce n'est plus une perception
Acquise, mais une perception
Confuse, I knows that I knows
What I knows that I knows,
Dat, no dit-dit-dit, dah-dah-dah,
Written only on the air, verbal
Strabismus, *στράβος,* STP,
Struggling scenery, slippery
And unfashionable, innumerable,
Too dimensional to be bearable,
Une collection d'unités, one
For all, all for once, seeking
La synthèse de l'un et du multiple,
Eh, maybe, maybe not, more
Knots and double knots, slip

Knots, and footless noting,
Nuttin' doin', *plus de charme*
À l'espérance qu'à la possession,
Au rêve qu'à la réalité, you askin'
Me or tellin' me, out the window,
Leaves aflutter in late afternoon
Lateral light, in depth perception,
Flattering natural light,
Slight breeze, breathy flight,
What, *mon ami,* are we to make
Of this, *cette lenitude,* there
And here, *cette infinité de possibles.*

23.
Scotographic analecta, aphasiatic,
Gustatory, haptic, what do I see
When I do not see what I see,
Ectoplasmic visuals, flat screen
Hallucinations, shady
Cavern shows, *la durée,* says
M. Blanc, *est de courte durée,*
Abuzz with attic wasps, sophismic,
That timid toe in that unique river,
Just rollin' along, or maybe it's the toe
That's unique, red, raw, hidden, stumped,
Nevertheless, never twice, nevermore,
Ravenous, hungry for troth, answer me
This, infolded sage, is that a sane
Sliver, a tame saw, towed scow,

Sowed tare, sewn tear, sorrow
And shame and always pity,
Always, piteous piety, pretty
Unsatisfactory, huh, knock, knock,
Try naming six senses, shut my mouth,
Ears, nose, fingertips, then what
Do I see when I can see nothing,
Who's there, what's where,
A seventh dwarf, daft and dopey,
Shout it out, that that you see
When they turn out the lights,
Stars like dust, optic occlusions,
Let's do the math, symbolic
Sufferance, things I have seen
Although I have not been
To where they are, haven't I heard
That somewhere, it's so familiar,
Les mots juste avant le nuit,
Blackout, blacked out, out cold,
Deletions, esemplastic erasures,
Entoptic osmosis, leakings out,
A livid swirl, what's the name
Of this game, *ce jeu, dieses Spiel,*
What are the rules, *les règles,*
And who is that man in the barrel
Who just snuffed out the lamp,
Or is it just another *solus rex,*
Solipsistic slip-n-slide, down
We go, hanging onto sight,

Your move or mine, a shot
In the eventide, let's just see
About that, why don't we,
Smell it out, touch base,
Listen close now, tastes
Bad, wouldn't eat that, most
Likely tainted with shigella,
E. coli, or something even worse,
Locally routed, almost surely fatal,
Say can you see what I'm saying,
No peeking, just sort it out,
There's a tooth in every joke,
A choke in every choice,
And what are ya gonna do
When the pride ebbs out
And leaves ya in the dark,
Toes sinking in the sound,
Stranded in the shadows,
Waiting for somebody
Finally to strap on the light.

24.

Solemn beliefs bring only brief
Relief, do you believe that,
If so, wherefore, this indigent
Imploration, this expeditious
Exploration, this querulous
Questioning, *woran wir glauben,*
Hängt von dem ab, was wir

Lernen, so, is that a squirrel there,
Dodging induction, or maybe
A duck, a rabbit, that's a corny
Question, I know, I do know, but
What isn't, abductive indentures,
Factional resistants, aw, believe
What you will, humph, so says
Inverately knotty Alexander,
Bain danseur of the Scottish real,
So long as you observe
These tense commitments,
If you know it, plow it,
If you plow it, sow it,
If you sow it, grow it,
If you grow it, mow it,
If you mow it, reap it,
If you reap it, stow it,
If you stow it, keep it,
If you keep it, strew it,
If you strew it, know it,
If you know it, do it,
And start all over again,
That's what we call
The jiggery poke, so what's
All that about, huh,
Sagt man eben dies,
Belief without doing
Ain't no believin' at all,
Is that it, seems so, it do,

But what do I know, crows
In the cornfield, withered
And sere, or maybe high
As an elephantine sigh,
Nice try, yes, yesterday
I watched two mockingbirds
Play tag in, through, around
The berried branches of
A holly tree until I had
To give it up, rabbiting
Around, squirreling
Whirlings, duckings
In and out in dubious
Prattle, flirtatious flittering,
Ocular vocality, silential
Flutter bys, until, oh get on
About it, say what you
Intend, quit all this sputtering
And stammering, uh, uh, uh,
Until I knew what I believed,
Believed what I knew,
Wenn ich der Evidenz
Nich traue, warum soll ich
Dann irgend Evidenz trauen,
Ain't that just so, fact to fact,
Not withstanding that sweet
Tripartite warble, that dauntless
Singalingaling, top tips of spruce,

As sun slides down verdant
Into western night noise.

25.

Thanatoptic *tropismes*, tropal
Topicalities, ectopic inquiries,
Θανάτος, every body's doin' it,
Doin' it, doin' it, all almost alike,
First four notes of body and soul,
Boredom and whoredom, *c'ést*
À mourir d'ennui, whose bitch
Are you, quarry-slave at night,
Scouring his donjon, last dangle
Dong of dum de dum dum, mos'
Nobody live to tell the toll,
Οβολός for the ferry fare,
Tip for the topper chop,
Penance for the bland, maybe
So, lid weights, light waits,
Il est vrai, qu'à en retarder
La chute, but so-so it goes,
Ground down, underground,
What a stinker, will the neighbors
Notice, like as not, oblivious
To oblivion, *der Tod ist kein*
Ereignis des Lebens, I gotcha,
But everybody's booin' it, chawin'
It, Eumolpan jerky-chewin' it,

Chokin' it down , chompin' it up,
Some load, whatta dump, can't we
Find some other place to squat,
Some well lit place without that
Blurry EXIT sign, some tomb
With a view, or that numinous
Caravan, synechistic continuity,
Ubertarian never-say-die,
I heard tell of that, tale beyond
Talent, *a u s s e r h a l b*
Von Raum und Zeit, universe
Not constructed to suit the scheme
Of some silly scold, so says
Charles Sanders, C. S. to you,
Oh, am I condescending, very well,
I am condescending, contentious,
Conversant, contradictorily
Concupiscible, condemnatorious,
And yet concrescive, concordable,
Herr Schwarz and M. Noir,
We're all in this together, mates,
Concorporeal, a mousy ovum
In every dermatoplast, each in each
One's own solitary cell, sentenced
Sans paroles, moot, wordless,
Up in a cloud of witlessness,
Caught, all altogether now, now
Recklessly redeemed, unclocked,
Insecure in our unknowing yet

Knock, knock, knocking, God
Sped to where we're going,
Never slowing, nowhere fast, fit
And fettled, I knows what I knows,
In indissoluble solation, *toutefois,*
Nevertheless, however, *doch,*
Ich das noch nicht sagen kann,
You got that, that what all this has
Been about, to speak that which
Is unparseable, to parse that which
Is unspeakable, with ineluctable
Acceptance of things that go
And then don't go, that come
But do not stay, you say it
For me, *ja, oui,* Mr. Shakes,
The rest is silence. O,o,o,o.

SILENCE

SILENCE

1′

2′
sharp ting,
ring on flat metal
rail

3′
Cage rouses
pleased at sound
looks around

4′
blood's slow hum
1,000 bodies
breath

4′ 33″
beyond all hearing

FACTORY
HOLLOW
PRESS

Hadley
Massachusetts